DAV

IMAGES
of America

OCALA NATIONAL
FOREST

IMAGES
of America

OCALA NATIONAL FOREST

Dr. Rob Norman
Foreword by Gene Gallant

Published by Arcadia Publishing
Charleston, South Carolina

Printed in the United States of America

Library of Congress Control Number: 2010929740

For all general information, please contact Arcadia Publishing:
Telephone 843-853-2070
Fax 843-853-0044
E-mail sales@arcadiapublishing.com
For customer service and orders:
Toll-Free 1-888-313-2665

Visit us on the Internet at www.arcadiapublishing.com

CONTENTS

FOREWORD

The Ocala National Forest, a vast, sprawling wilderness area that encompasses some 362,000 acres interspersed with numerous lakes, rivers, streams, and springs, has been home to mankind for at least 10,000 years.

Numerous archaeological sites have been discovered within its confines. Artifacts and relics of the past attest to the numerous cultures that have called it home.

Following the Second Seminole War (1835–1842) and the American Civil War (1861–1865), the forest, affectionately called the "Big Scrub" by its pioneer inhabitants, has played a prominent role in the history of the North-Central Florida region. The vast stands of cypress, pine, and cedar drew loggers, sawmills, and related businesses to its depths, and in turn, railroads, riverboats, and river ports became a vital part of our history.

The huge stretches of rich hammock lands and fertile flood-plain areas drew scores of farmers from other sections of the South, resulting in new settlements with schools, churches, and a network of roads.

From the first Native Americans to the modern-day vacationer, the forest has been a magnet that has drawn people to its resources, beauty, and recreational activities in ever-increasing numbers. Let us hope that the magnet never loses its power and that the Ocala National Forest will forever remain a vital part of our heritage.

—Gene Gallant

Gene Gallant is a fifth-generation Marion County "cracker." His great-grandfather homesteaded in the "Big Scrub" area in the 1840s. Much of his love of history was a result of many hours spent listening to his grandmother and great-grandfather talk of their early lives spent in the pioneer environment of Marion County. He is the author of eight books about Florida's and Marion County's history, which includes three books on pioneer cooking and Civil War cooking. Other topics that Gallant has written about include Florida's Second Seminole War, the history of steam boating on the Ocklawaha and Silver Rivers, and Civil War poetry.

He is currently working on a book that will cover the following subjects: a brief history of Marion County just prior to the Civil War; the Civil War military units organized in the county; the Reconstruction Era; the beginning of the timber and logging industries that flourished along the Ocklawaha River; farming and early industry, including sawmills and lime rock and phosphate mining; and events leading up to the beginning of World War II.

ACKNOWLEDGMENTS

Thanks to the many individuals that I interviewed for this book, including Richard Mills and Gene Gallant, and all the editors at Arcadia Publishing.

Thanks to God for creating such a magical place as the Ocala National Forest. Much love to my wife, Carol, and my family and friends for all their support with my writing. And a special thanks goes to Ibsen A. Morales for his help in editing the book.

INTRODUCTION

And here were forests ancient as the hills, Enfolding sunny spots of greenery.

—Samuel Taylor Coleridge, *Kubla Khan*

To take on a project as big and vast as the Ocala National Forest is monumental. I look at the forest as the stage of an enormous and ever-changing ecological theatre onto which untold numbers of lives have come and gone. My questions include the following: What makes up the stage? How do characters come and go on this stage? How and why has this happened?

Major river arteries, primarily north and south with the Ocklawaha fed by the Silver Springs run and the St. Johns River, have allowed visitors to enter here. Now highway interstates allow major interactions along both margins of the forest and more forays inside the forest. Today the Ocala National Forest—a popular recreation area for canoeing, swimming, camping, hiking, picnicking, and hunting—receives more visitors than any other national forest in the Sunshine State. Millions of visitors annually escape to this forest, which is one of Central Florida's last remaining traces of forested land.

Ocala National Forest is the oldest national forest east of the Mississippi River and the southernmost in the nation. On November 24, 1908, Pres. Theodore Roosevelt signed the original proclamation establishing the Ocala National Forest, reserving it from public domain lands. The forest has numerous threatened and endangered species, and management is geared to protect and perpetuate these species. The sand pine scrub is the largest in the world. Juniper Springs Recreation Area, dedicated in 1936, has been in continuous use since its dedication.

The following is a partial quote from the proclamation: "Do proclaim that there are hereby reserved from settlement or entry and set apart as a public reservation, for the use and benefit of the people, all the tracts of land, in the State of Florida, shown as the Ocala National Forest." This proclamation in 1908 reserved this land for the "use and benefit of the people." On July 16, 1938, Pres. Franklin D. Roosevelt established the Ocala National Forest boundary.

What are the origins of the word *Ocala*? Some say it is a Timucuan-Indian term meaning "fair land" or "big hammock." More generally accepted is that Ocala is believed to have come from the name of a Native American chief called Ocali, who was in the area around 1539. The history of the First Peoples settling in the forest is as indefinite as the boundaries of the land.

Imagine being in the forest 10 million years ago during the Pliocene and Miocene eras. You take a walk. With each step forward, you may see giant raccoons and scores of other ungulates or hoofed animals. When you get deeper into the woods, you may think you were walking around today. The cypress, conifers, magnolias, and palms have a similar appearance now, as they did when the giraffe-camels ate freely from the tall branches and giant vegetarian sloths hugged the trees. Above you fly anhingas, grebes, and dragonflies, and you may spot an armadillo that looks like the greatest-grandfather to one of today's ground sniffers.

You will, however, never spot a dinosaur; the great peninsula of Florida was underwater when they thundered across other lands. During these periods of submersion, mollusks and fish swept in from the sea, leaving a legacy of countless shells and bones when they perished. The calcium content of the marine life was the primary ingredient of the limestone foundation that is millions of years old. The rising and cracking of the limestone crust formed the ridges running down the center of the peninsula. Relic dunes appeared following submersion.

Keep walking—Ocala's ridges, being slightly higher than the coastal regions, were the first to dry out, which became an island of refuge for semiaquatic creatures and other animals. Even the remnants of beached whales are still discovered. Following the retreat of the glaciers, the vegetation returned. Acidic water crept into the limestone, creating subterranean caves and fissures. Empty spaces were soon filled with rainwater, which helped to erode the rock, and the new woods, made of a collection of sand, twigs, and leaves, took shape and filled in the openings. As the water lowered, new caves were carved as well as curved passages. With the passing of time, the rain pushed bones, fossils, shells, soil, and leaves down into the lower caves, carrying liquid organic acid to dissolve the underlying bedrocks. Sinkholes were formed in the upper caves.

Look around—snowy egrets flaunt their breeding plumage and high-step through the aquatic vegetation, showing off the bright yellow feet that give them the nickname of "little golden slippers." Turkey vultures perch on the top fronds of cabbage watching the neighborhood, and ibis, cormorants, and osprey join storks, herons, and anhingas in the competition for fish. Bass break the water's surface in search of food. Sandhill cranes fly overhead, deer graze in the shallows, and alligators line the river and lakes like ancient sentinels. Coots, with their unmistakable white bills and plaintive calls, common moorhens, and lesser scaups mingle and feed. You will observe that the forest and surrounding area supports an abundance of wildlife.

In her wonderful book *Forest in the Sand*, Marjory Bartlett Sanger writes, "Every forest has its own story to tell. It tells of the years it has seen and its beginnings and how it has grown old with the earth. It tells of the plants and animals living in it, its sunshine and winds and rains, its seasons and cuttings and dyings and renewals. Like the ocean, the forest is in a state of constant movement, rising and falling, growing and diminishing, never at rest."

One

HISTORY OF THE FOREST

SKELETON UNEARTHED, SILVER GLEN SPRINGS. The periods of study in the forest include the Paleo, Archaic, Transitional (from Archaic to Woodland), Woodland, Contact Period, and then the historic periods. Native Americans have lived in Florida for at least 12,000 years, and many changes have occurred in their tools, ornaments, and way of life. (Courtesy of Henderson Library.)

STONE AGE TOOLS DISCOVERED, SILVER GLEN SPRINGS. Native Americans lived in the St. Johns River area since about 5,000 years ago, as shown by radiocarbon dating of shell mounds scattered along the river. The mounds apparently were built close to the water where the snails lived. Since they were formed, the water has cut deeper into the riverbed, leaving the mounds up to a half a mile from the St. Johns River. (Courtesy of Henderson Library.)

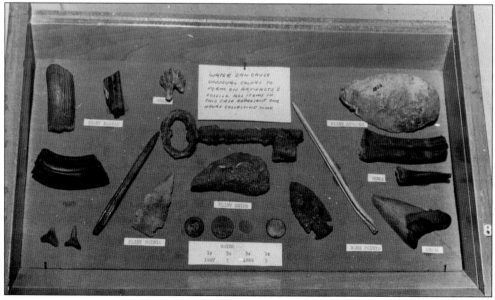

MORE ARTIFACTS. The main evidence of Native American life in this area is the large shell middens or mounds or garbage heaps. Native Americans discarding the small snail shells that served as the mainstay in their diets formed these over hundreds or thousands of years. (Courtesy of Silver River Museum.)

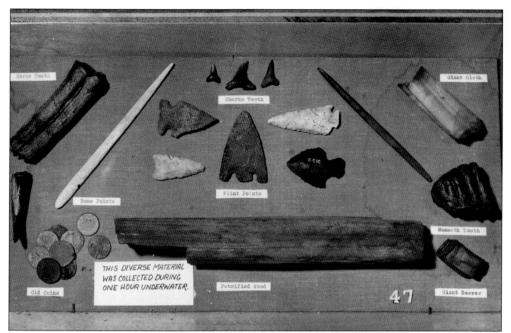

DIVERSE MATERIAL COLLECTED. The 12 known mounds on national forest land vary in size from about 4 feet high and 50 feet long up to 19 feet high and 400 feet long. (Courtesy of Henderson Library.)

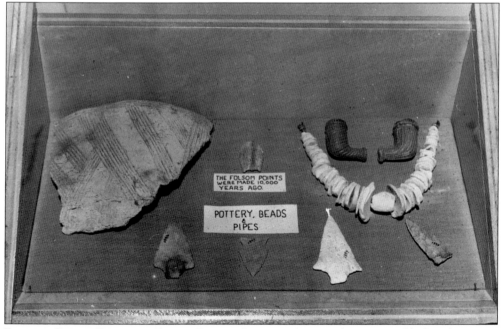

POTTERY, BEADS, PIPES, AND FOLSOM POINTS. Portions of a mound constructed before the Native Americans learned to make pottery contained few artifacts other than shells, pieces of bone, and scattered projectile points. In later periods, starting from about 1,400 BCE, the mounds began to contain a wealth of pottery sherds, bone pipes, little shells, and fire hearth. (Courtesy of Silver River Museum.)

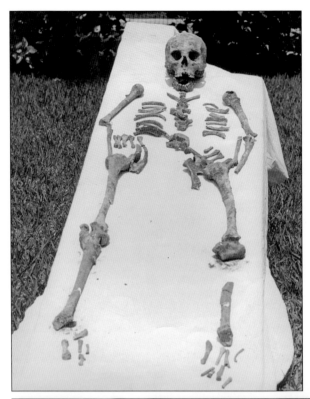

SKELETAL REMAINS, SILVER GLEN SPRINGS. Paleo-Indian sites that are about 12,000 years old have been unearthed, which makes the Paleo Indians the first inhabitants of the forest. Three Spanish missions are known to have existed in the 16th century, and currently a mission bell is on display in the Silver River Museum. Although the earliest pre-contact evidence has been dated to about 12,000 years ago, it is more likely that the Native Americans had lived here prior to that time. (Both courtesy of Henderson Library.)

ARROWHEADS AND DEATH POINTS, SILVER GLEN SPRINGS. Around 2,000 years ago, the Native Americans developed the bow and arrow, raised crops, and utilized sand burial mounds. This was the Transitional Period, which was also a time of farming. When Europeans first arrived in this area in the 16th century, the inhabitants were Timucuan Indians. Now, however, the population consisted of Seminoles, who were Creek Indians; African Americans, who were escaped slaves; and other indigenous Native American tribes such as the Timucuan. (Courtesy of Henderson Library.)

FOLSOM POINTS. The post-contact cultures also included Native Americans in missions and Seminoles. The missions converted many Native Americans to Catholicism ("missionized" Native Americans), and the population was then composed of Catholics and Native Americans with their "pagan" beliefs. After fighting in a war in Alabama, the Creek Indians moved into Florida along with assimilated slaves. (Courtesy of Silver River Museum.)

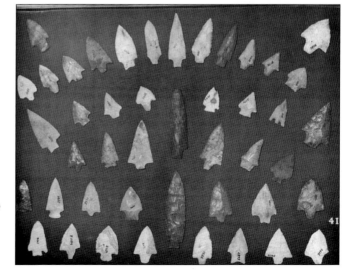

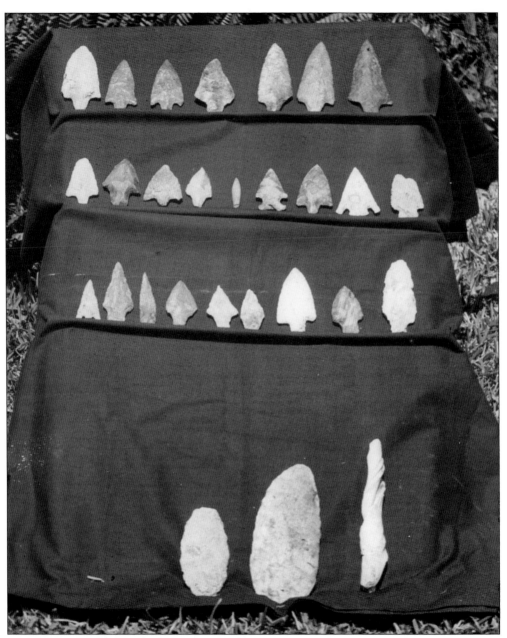

ARTIFACTS ON DISPLAY. The first record of white visitation to the area of Marion County occurred when Hernando De Soto in 1539 explored the Florida region. During his travels, he encountered a large settlement of Timucuan Indians in a region called Ocali. Trading relationships were noted from 1600 to 1656 with Spanish missions on the Ocklawaha River. When American settlers began to inhabit the Florida Territory after 1821, U.S. government authorities acknowledged the serious problem of Native American removal. Due to "the inadequacy of the Florida reservation and the desperate situation of the Seminoles living there, plus the mounting demand on their removal," the Treaty of Paynes Landing was formulated in 1832 to persuade the Native Americans to migrate west. A few tribes agreed to the provisions of the treaty, but many did not; such conflict soon led to the outbreak of the Second Seminole War. (Courtesy of Henderson Museum.)

Skeleton Unearthed
of
Silver Glen Springs
Florida

© Silver Glen Springs
Corporation

ARCHAEOLOGICAL DIG, SILVER GLEN SPRINGS. Ripley Bullen was also active on the west side of the forest and published the results of his excavations conducted at Sunday Bluff in 1969. Materials associated with the Sunday Bluff excavations are presently curated at the Florida Museum of Natural History in Gainesville. The Ocala National Forest has been the subject of a number of archeological investigations over the last 150 years, and there are over 100 sites recorded within the forest boundaries. (Both courtesy of Henderson Museum.)

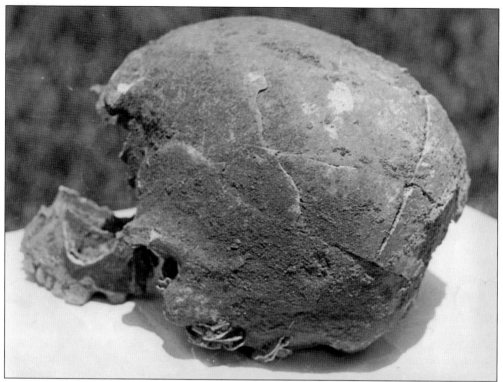

SKULLS FOUND, SILVER GLEN SPRINGS. At the time of contact, the Timucuan Indians inhabited the St. Johns River basin. By the late 18th century, they had been completely removed from the area and were sparsely replaced by the Seminoles until the end of the Seminole Wars in the 1840s. (Courtesy of Henderson Museum.)

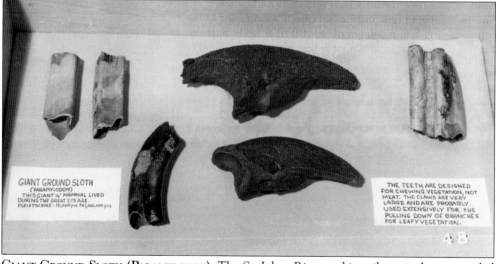

GIANT GROUND SLOTH
(PARAMYLODON)
THIS GIANT 14' MAMMAL LIVED
DURING THE GREAT ICE AGE.
PLEISTOCENE - 10,000 yrs To 1,000,000 yrs

THE TEETH ARE DESIGNED
FOR CHEWING VEGETATION, NOT
MEAT. THE CLAWS ARE VERY
LARGE AND ARE PROBABLY
USED EXTENSIVELY FOR THE
PULLING DOWN OF BRANCHES
FOR LEAFY VEGETATION.

GIANT GROUND SLOTH (PARAMYLODON). The St. Johns River and its tributaries have provided access to the interior of Florida for at least 4,000 years, and it is not surprising that the earliest archeological investigations focused on the St. Johns area. Prior to 1900, Jeffries Wyman and Clarence B. Moore were the principal investigators of archeological work within the Ocala National Forest. (Courtesy of Henderson Museum.)

JEFF WYMAN. In 1875, acclaimed archaeologist Jefferies Wyman published his study, "Fresh-water Shell Mounds of the St. Johns River, Florida." Wyman examined midden mounds throughout the entire river system, ending at the "Bear Midden," which is south of Puzzle Lake, near Cone Lake (near present day Highway 50). Wyman was distinguished for being the first scientist to understand that the shell mounds were human made and not the result of natural events. (Courtesy of Henderson Museum.)

MAMMOTH TEETH. The Paleo-Indian tradition is the earliest prehistoric occupation and most poorly represented cultural period in the forest area; however, a verified mammoth kill site has been recorded on Silver Springs Run, just west of the forest. Silver Springs Run, less than 8 kilometers in length, is a primary tributary of the Ocklawaha River. The relative proximity of the Silver Springs Run site to the Ocklawaha, a similar environment, strengthens the possibility of Paleo-Indian sites being located within the forest. (Courtesy of Silver River Museum.)

19

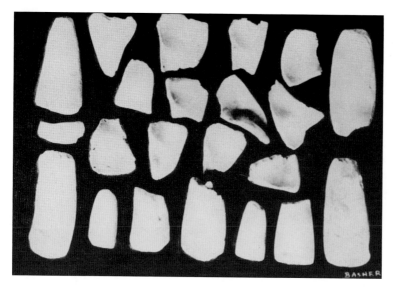

Spoon and Celts Discovered, Silver Glen Springs. The Mission Indians died out by the 1750s, and then the Creek Indians came in. They often intermarried with the former slaves. The Seminole Indian Wars (1836–1841) came and changed the world of Florida. (Courtesy of Henderson Library.)

Stone Age Relics, Silver Glen Springs. From the conventional starting point of 12,000 to 9,000 years ago, the Paleo Indians inhabited the forest. The Archaic Period began, and the ice age ended with the megafauna extinct. The nomadic lifestyle turned in a slow progression during the Archaic Period of 9,000 to 4,000 years ago. The pottery discovered 4,000 years ago was the event that terminated the period, and the Native Americans settled into villages and farms. (Courtesy of Henderson Library.)

DIPPER, MAUL, AND OTHER STONE AGE TOOLS, SILVER GLEN SPRINGS, 1995. About 4,000 years ago, pottery was invented in the St. Johns River area that is probably 80 years earlier than the occurrence of pottery in any other part of the country. The first pottery was tempered with fibrous materials—shredded palmetto fiber, Spanish moss, and grass. The fiber was ground up and mixed with clay. Later in the sand-tempered method, a small amount of large-grained (1/6 inch) sand was added to the clay mix. The Bible speaks of instances when the ancient people did not have straw to temper the bricks that they were making. This is analogous to the fiber used in this area. Many of the mounds in the forest were created and abandoned before pottery was invented and, thus, are devoid of any pottery artifacts. Later Native Americans who camped on the high ground offered by the mounds probably dropped these potsherds. (Courtesy of Henderson Library.)

STONE AGE POTTERY, SILVER GLEN SPRINGS, 1987. Over a period of thousands of years, the Native Americans improved their pottery-making skills, and gradually the pots became rounded. Later pots often had concentric diamonds incised into the sides that suggest they were copying basket patterns. Two methods of moulding the clay were employed. Large pots were made by rolling out long strands of clay about a quarter inch in diameter, and then beginning at the bottom center of the bowl the strand of clay was coiled around, stacking one coil upon another. The Native Americans then used their fingers to pinch or bond the various layers of clay coils together. A wooden paddle was used to beat the clay and form it into a compact mass. The complete pot was allowed to sit for a day or two until it lost enough moisture to harden. Supported by sticks, it was placed upside down and roasted over a fire until all the moisture was driven out. The first pots were shaped with flat bottoms and straight sides, very similar to the baskets Native Americans used. (Courtesy of Henderson Library.)

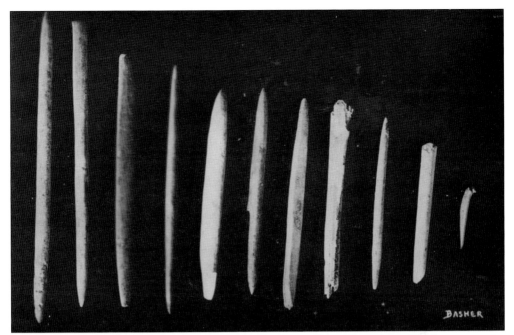

STONE AGE NEEDLES AND AWLS, SILVER GLEN SPRINGS. The generalized cultural sequence for the Ocala National Forest area encompasses a time span from approximately 12,000 BCE to the present. The sequence is divided into two sections, prehistoric and historic. Prehistory refers to any cultural expression from the time of human entry into Florida until European contact. Historic refers to any cultural activity after European contact. (Courtesy of Henderson Library.)

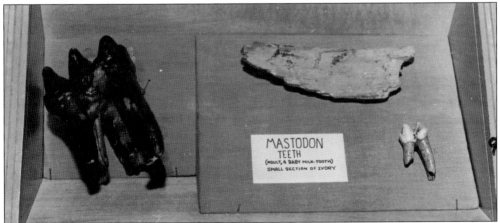

MASTODON TEETH AND IVORY. Pictured here from left to right are an adult tooth, a small section of ivory, and a baby milk tooth. Physical evidence of this Paleo-Indian Period in Florida is scant for several reasons. During the early Paleo-Indian Period, sea level was as much as 30 to 35 meters (100–115 feet) lower than in the present. Small human bands entered a much larger Florida peninsula. The First Peoples probably briefly occupied campsites located along freshwater sources (most often flowing streams or springs). After exploiting (hunting and gathering) the immediate environment, they would move to another area of water and fresh resources. It is also surmised that people followed migrating Pleistocene megafauna, such as mammoth, mastodon, and ground sloth. Small groups would have made use of huge tracts of land to support themselves. (Courtesy of Silver River Museum.)

Bone Hairpins, Tools, and Projectiles. Most of the mounds contain other types of artifacts like stone projectile points; scrapers; tools; conch shells, which were used for axes and hoes; bone; pins, which were used for perforating skins; or needles for drilling holes. Materials such as wooden handles, arrow shafts, and clothing cannot be found since these materials rotted long ago. (Courtesy of Silver River Museum.)

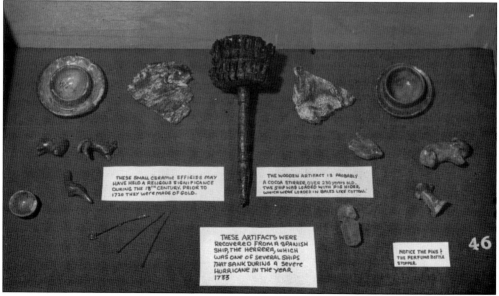

Small Ceramic Effigies, Wooden Artifact, Pins, and Perfume Bottle Stoppers. Apparently the mounds were not built to be burial mounds as other Native Americans did, but skeletons are sometimes found in them. By analyzing the artifacts found in the mounds, archaeologists are able to show the patterns of trade between various surrounding tribes that built up as material, such as stone and pottery from certain locations, gradually increased in concentration in the mounds. (Courtesy of Silver River Museum.)

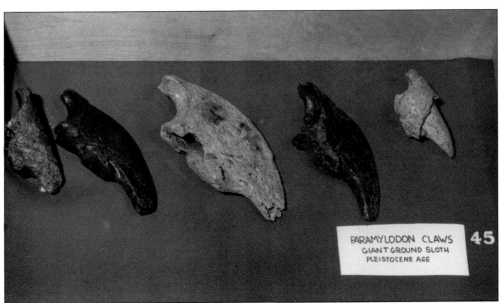

PARAMYLODON CLAWS
GIANT GROUND SLOTH
PLEISTOCENE AGE

45

GIANT GROUND SLOTH CLAWS, PLEISTOCENE AGE. The Early Archaic Period, from 9,000 to 6,000 years ago, represents a cultural and environmental transition between the Paleo Indian and the Middle Archaic, which is usually referred to as Classic Archaic. Dryer environmental conditions created a shift in the exploitation of large game animals to the hunting of modern game animals such as deer, bear, and bison. A continued rise in sea level during this period resulted in a smaller Florida land mass and increased competition for resources. (Courtesy of Silver River Museum.)

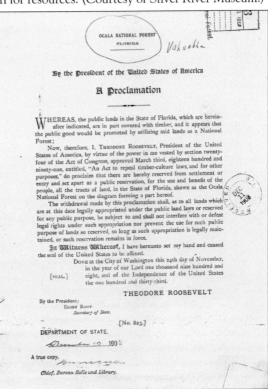

OCALA NATIONAL FOREST PROCLAMATION. In the late 1800s, publications that described Marion and Lake Counties as "tropical paradises" were dispersed nationally to encourage migration to the area. Most of the promotions centered on the Ocala-Silver Springs region and not the Big Scrub. However, in 1908, Florida congressman Herbert L. Anderson, who realized the importance in saving this vast wilderness, succeeded in having Congress declare the region between the St. Johns and Ocklawaha Rivers a national forest, and Theodore Roosevelt signed the bill on December 8, 1908. (Courtesy of Richard Mills.)

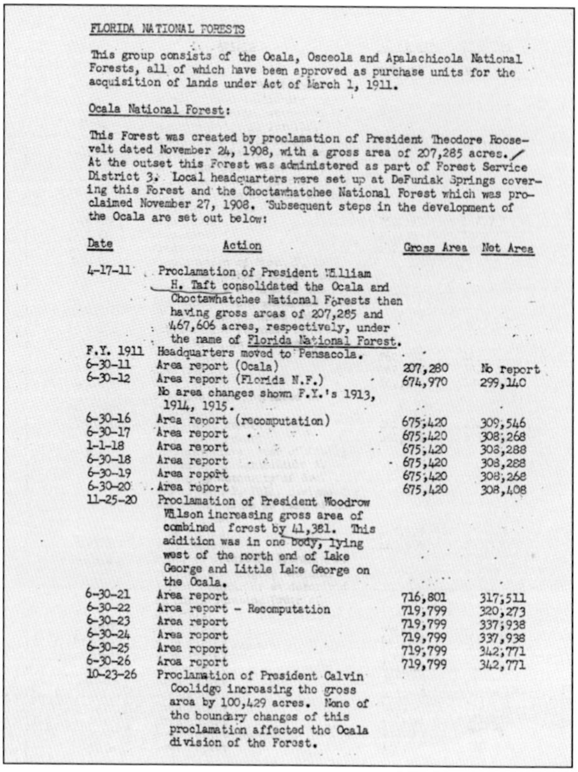

FLORIDA NATIONAL FORESTS

This group consists of the Ocala, Osceola and Apalachicola National Forests, all of which have been approved as purchase units for the acquisition of lands under Act of March 1, 1911.

Ocala National Forest:

This Forest was created by proclamation of President Theodore Roosevelt dated November 24, 1908, with a gross area of 207,285 acres. At the outset this Forest was administered as part of Forest Service District 3. Local headquarters were set up at DeFuniak Springs covering this Forest and the Choctawhatchee National Forest which was proclaimed November 27, 1908. Subsequent steps in the development of the Ocala are set out below:

Date	Action	Gross Area	Net Area
4-17-11	Proclamation of President William H. Taft consolidated the Ocala and Choctawhatchee National Forests then having gross areas of 207,285 and 467,606 acres, respectively, under the name of Florida National Forest.		
F.Y. 1911	Headquarters moved to Pensacola.		
6-30-11	Area report (Ocala)	207,280	No report
6-30-12	Area report (Florida N.F.)	674,970	299,140
	No area changes shown F.Y.'s 1913, 1914, 1915.		
6-30-16	Area report (recomputation)	675,420	309,546
6-30-17	Area report	675,420	308,268
1-1-18	Area report	675,420	308,288
6-30-18	Area report	675,420	308,288
6-30-19	Area report	675,420	308,268
6-30-20	Area report	675,420	308,408
11-25-20	Proclamation of President Woodrow Wilson increasing gross area of combined forest by 41,381. This addition was in one body, lying west of the north end of Lake George and Little Lake George on the Ocala.		
6-30-21	Area report	716,801	317,511
6-30-22	Area report - Recomputation	719,799	320,273
6-30-23	Area report	719,799	337,938
6-30-24	Area report	719,799	337,938
6-30-25	Area report	719,799	342,771
6-30-26	Area report	719,799	342,771
10-23-26	Proclamation of President Calvin Coolidge increasing the gross area by 100,429 acres. None of the boundary changes of this proclamation affected the Ocala division of the Forest.		

HISTORIC DOCUMENTS OF THE FOREST. On March 3, 1845, Florida was granted statehood. Congress later granted 500,000 acres of land to the state for "internal improvements." In 1850, the federal government conveyed the titles to 20 million acres of sovereign lands and wetlands to the State of Florida through an act that transferred all "land unfit for cultivation due to its swampy and overflowed condition." Wetlands throughout the state were drained to maximize agricultural and residential development. Florida's population reached 140,000 in 1860. (Both courtesy of Richard Mills.)

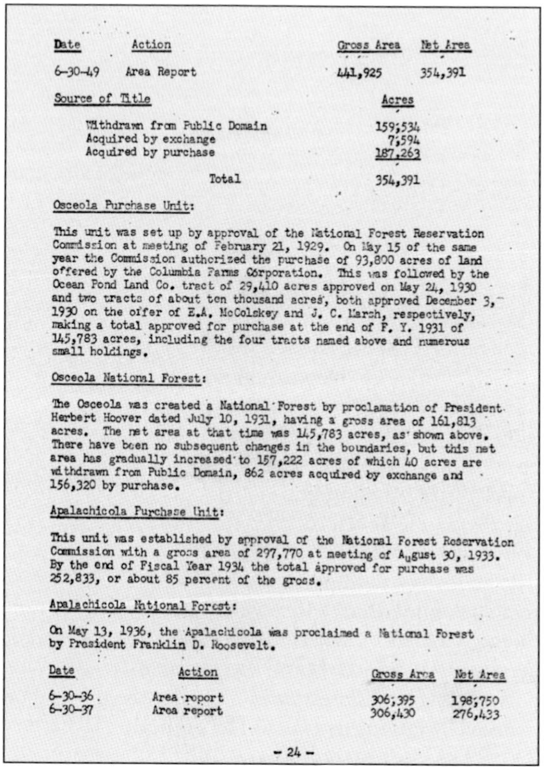

Date	Action	Gross Area	Net Area
6-30-49	Area Report	441,925	354,391

Source of Title		Acres
Withdrawn from Public Domain		159,534
Acquired by exchange		7,594
Acquired by purchase		187,263
Total		354,391

Osceola Purchase Unit:

This unit was set up by approval of the National Forest Reservation Commission at meeting of February 21, 1929. On May 15 of the same year the Commission authorized the purchase of 93,800 acres of land offered by the Columbia Farms Corporation. This was followed by the Ocean Pond Land Co. tract of 29,410 acres approved on May 24, 1930 and two tracts of about ten thousand acres, both approved December 3, 1930 on the offer of E.A. McColskey and J. C. Marsh, respectively, making a total approved for purchase at the end of F. Y. 1931 of 145,783 acres, including the four tracts named above and numerous small holdings.

Osceola National Forest:

The Osceola was created a National Forest by proclamation of President Herbert Hoover dated July 10, 1931, having a gross area of 161,813 acres. The net area at that time was 145,783 acres, as shown above. There have been no subsequent changes in the boundaries, but this net area has gradually increased to 157,222 acres of which 40 acres are withdrawn from Public Domain, 862 acres acquired by exchange and 156,320 by purchase.

Apalachicola Purchase Unit:

This unit was established by approval of the National Forest Reservation Commission with a gross area of 297,770 at meeting of August 30, 1933. By the end of Fiscal Year 1934 the total approved for purchase was 252,833, or about 85 percent of the gross.

Apalachicola National Forest:

On May 13, 1936, the Apalachicola was proclaimed a National Forest by President Franklin D. Roosevelt.

Date	Action	Gross Area	Net Area
6-30-36	Area report	306,395	198,750
6-30-37	Area report	306,430	276,433

Two

SHAPED BY
WATER AND FIRE

RIVER IN THE FOREST. The St. Johns is the largest river in the Florida peninsula, and with the Ocklawaha it shares the hydrologic distinction of flowing northward. The Ocklawaha has its source in the system of large lakes (Griffin, Eusris, Dora, Harris, and Apopka) in the central area of the peninsula and flows northerly, then eastwardly, emptying into the St. Johns River in the vicinity of Welaka, some 22 miles south of Palatka. The drainage area is about 750 square miles. Here is a view of the waterways at Ocala National Park. (Courtesy of State Library and Archives of Florida and the U.S. Forest Service.)

PADDLING A WATERWAY. Hydrologically, the forest is highly diversified. Over 600 lakes and ponds are located within the forest boundary. The Ocala also contains the only first magnitude spring in U.S. Forest Service ownership (Alexander Springs). In addition, five of the seven publicly owned second magnitude springs are found within the forest. These are Juniper, Fern Hammock, Fernandez, Salt, and one unnamed spring. (Both courtesy of Marion County Public Library System.)

CANOEING AT JUNIPER SPRINGS, 1966. Pictured from left to right are Jim Perry, Judy Perry, Nancy Brower, and Bill Brower. (Photograph by Johnson; courtesy of State Library and Archives of Florida and the U.S. Forest Service.)

SALT SPRINGS. Salt Springs's recreational area is on the shores of a beautiful natural spring, which empties into Lake George, the state's second-largest lake. Vents of salt and freshwater flow into the spring, which creates a distortion of objects underwater known as a halocline. This feature, unique to Salt Springs, makes it a favorite among snorkelers and swimmers. The 5-mile run is ideal for canoeing, boating, and fishing. (Courtesy of Richard Mills.)

WOMEN ENJOYING THE COOL WATERS. Renowned as one of the best recreational areas in the region, with a flow of 20 million gallons of water a day, Juniper Springs has a 7-mile canoe run with a wealth of wildlife en route that includes otters, deer, and bird life. The campground at Juniper Springs is in such demand that reservations are not accepted, and accommodations are handled on a first-come basis. (Courtesy of State Library and Archives of Florida.)

PADDLING THROUGH NARROW WAYS. Alexander Springs pumps out 76 million gallons of warm water each day of the year, which flows into Alexander Creek. Canoeists use this run for excursions into the unspoiled forest, and the spring is so large that local scuba experts use it for new diving certification tests. The spring is encircled by a nature trail that winds through the forest, and swimmers and sunbathers make good use of the large sand beach. (Courtesy of Marion County Public Library System.)

GROUPS OF PEOPLE CANOEING, JUNIPER SPRINGS, 1980. The 7-mile canoe run from Juniper Springs is one of the best canoeing opportunities in central Florida. The canopied creek winds through dense, primeval forests that seem untouched by man—on weekdays, anyway. Come early in the morning, and a person can paddle through dappled light that filters through the trees down into crystalline water. At first glance, the run looks too narrow to navigate, but it grows in size steadily as it meanders past ancient cypress trees and lush, semitropical forests. The narrow creek is filled with obstacles, and it takes some effort to avoid submerged snags and squeeze under overhanging branching. Whether a canoer finds it fun or frustrating may depend on the skill level. (Courtesy of State Library and Archives of Florida.)

PADDLING ON BEAUTIFUL WATERS, JUNIPER RUN. Juniper Springs Run is considered one of the top 25 canoeing spots in North America. It is a 7-mile run fed by 13 million gallons of crystal-clear water per day from Juniper and Fern Hammock Springs. The run takes four to five hours to complete. The upper portion is forested, narrow, shallow, and winding with some challenging obstacles, whereas the lower portion has multiple channels through an open, grassy prairie. (Courtesy of Marion County Public Library System.)

FISHING OFF THE DAM. In 1868, Florida's first water pollution law established a penalty for defiling or corrupting springs and water supplies. By 1870, Jacksonville had become a major port for lumber production and export. Hamilton Disston was credited with building canals across Central and Southern Florida to drain lands for agriculture. The Board of Trustees of the State Internal Improvement Trust Fund conveyed 4 million acres in Central and South Florida to Hamilton Disston of Philadelphia on the condition that he drain land to attract agricultural development. Disston worked until 1889 and succeeded in constructing canals between several of the Kissimmee chain of lakes and between the Caloosahatchee River and Lake Okeechobee. (Courtesy of State Library and Archives of Florida.)

FISHERMEN WITH THEIR CATCH. Oklawaha River largemouth bass fishing is good using live shiners and plastic worms around deepwater structures, while topwater lures are productive near vegetation and brush. Channel and white catfish are active downstream of Rodman Dam in deep holes along bends of the river and are taken on worms and chicken livers. Some crappies are caught on minnows around submerged brush. (Courtesy of State Library and Archives of Florida.)

CANOEING ON THE RIVER. Silver Glen Springs is a beautiful, 1,000-acre area bordering a crystal-clear spring, which makes it a good place for hiking, picnicking, bird watching, swimming, boating, or fishing. (Courtesy of State Library and Archives of Florida.)

VIEW FROM LOOKOUT TOWER. For tens of thousands of years, fire has been an important part of natural Florida. Long before man arrived, lightning started fires in Florida's woodlands and prairies. When the Native Americans came, they set fires to aid travel and to enhance hunting and farming. Fire is one of the most important natural processes in helping to preserve existing sand hills and natural communities. Natural lightning fires can no longer burn vast areas of Florida due to development and other cultural factors. (Courtesy of Marion County Public Library System.)

FOREST FIRE CARTOON. Since its vegetation has grown wild and lightning has fired up its skies, Florida has experienced fires on a cycle of every three to five years. Florida's fires received national media attention in the 1920s, which lead to the creation of the Florida Division of Forestry. The 1935 Big Scrub fire in the Ocala National Forest was the fastest spreading fire in the history of the United States, covering 35,000 acres in 4 hours. In 1935, twenty-one miles of forest were scorched between the Ocklawaha River and Lake George. (Courtesy of Richard Mills.)

IMPASSABLE BAY FIRE, 1955. In two hours, the 1955 fire had burned inside the forest. Fire lines were being plowed when the wind shifted, cutting off the line of retreat to Road 37. Brantley Graser, Ted Lasher, and Calvin Green were trapped, and Green ended up badly burned. The fire burned over 2,120 acres, damaging 5,069,847 board feet of timber valued at $105,000. It was sold for salvage and brought in $60,000. (Courtesy of State Library and Archives of Florida.)

SCRUB SEEN FROM FIRE OBSERVATION TOWER, 1927. The Ocala National Forest contains the largest continuous growth of sand pine (*Pinus clausa*) in the world, totaling 190,555 acres (51 percent of the total forest). The scrub qualifies as the largest single ecozone within the forest. The typical second-story growth includes the following: myrtle oak (*Quercus myrtifolia*), scrub live oak (*Quercus turbinella*), saw palmetto (*Serenoa repens*), rosemary (*Ceratiola ericoides*), and reindeer moss (*Cladonia spp.*). Moisture retention is extremely low and organic nutrients are quickly leached from the surface horizon. Daily summer temperatures in the scrub are higher than any other zone within the forest. The scrub served primarily as a zone of transportation with a secondary use for resource exploitation (perhaps for coontie [*Zamia tubers*]) for both prehistoric and historic populations. Remains of historic transportation routes (Volusia Trail, Churchill Road, Fort Gates Road, and the Fort King Road) traverse the scrub regions. (Photograph by James Hart Curry Martens; courtesy of State Library and Archives of Florida.)

SAW PALMETTO. The growth of a saw palmetto in the hammock means the area was once an open prairie or pine flatwoods. When lightning fires are suppressed for many years, prairies and flatwoods are unnaturally transformed into hammocks. As areas are "protected" from fires, the ability to be ignited diminishes, as does the likelihood of a fire spreading. (Courtesy of Marion County Public Library System.)

MARSHLAND AT OCALA NATIONAL PARK. The topography allows for a wide variety of environments and consists of highlands, coastal lowlands, swamps, springs, lakes, and ponds. Vegetation ranges from lush subtropical to prairie. Towering palms, large live oaks, and sand pines dominate the forest's scrub oak ecosystem. In the areas with more moisture, hardwoods thrive along with longleaf and slash pines. (Courtesy of State Library and Archives of Florida.)

PLANT OF OPUNTIA AMMOPHILA, 1918. Photographed on edge of prairie in Ocala National Forest is a young cactus plant. (Photograph by John Kunkel Small; courtesy of State Library and Archives of Florida.)

SILVER SPRINGS RUN AT OCKLAWAHA. The Oklawaha River Aquatic Preserve is made up of roughly 30 miles of the Oklawaha River system. The upper 5 miles of river were widened and straightened to some degree years ago to allow for navigation by larger vessels. The now defunct Cross Florida Barge Canal would have passed through these areas. About 5 miles downriver of the start of the preserve, the Oklawaha River meets the Silver River Spring run. This run is one of the largest spring runs in Florida, rivaling Rainbow Spring. It has an average discharge of over 500 million gallons a day. Over 3 miles of the roughly 5-mile run are part of the preserve. The headspring area is a tourist attraction. The next 20 miles of the Oklawaha River, downriver of this confluence, follow a narrow winding course. It is a black water river with a swamp canopy along most of its length. High areas meet the river intermittently to form sandy bluffs. The lock structure that was intended to flood the river as part of the Cross Florida Barge Canal still remains at the northern end of the preserve. (Courtesy of Marion County.)

Three

INHABITANTS AND NATURAL COMMUNITIES

LOOKING OUT TO LAKE KERR. The forest remained virtually untouched, except for the occasional visits of game hunters, until the 1930s. A method was devised that made sand pine a feasible source of pulpwood, which helped to increase logging operations in the forest. Also, in order to help alleviate the Depression, the Civilian Conservation Corps (CCC) hired persons to construct various recreational facilities in the forest. The CCC also excavated portions of the forest. The Depression hindered the tourist industry in the 1930s, and World War II also decreased tourism in the early 1940s. The second half of the 20th century brought many new residents to the region. Private lands were developed along the outskirts of the forest, but the Big Scrub still remains in a fairly pristine state. (Courtesy of U.S. Forest Service.)

LYNNE LOOKOUT TOWER, EASTERN DIVISION, 1935. The Ocala National Forest is a dynamic system involving the interplay between its natural features and the peoples who have come to occupy it. (Courtesy of Richard Mills.)

HOPKINS CATTLE AND PRAIRIE, 1928. Approximately 11percent (20,000 acres) of the sand pine scrub has been inventoried for cultural resources. No significant prehistoric or historic sites have been identified within this zone, indicating that the probability of these properties is extremely low. The scrub served primarily as a zone of transportation with a secondary use of resource exploitation for both prehistoric and historic populations. (Photograph by A. M. Kent; courtesy of Marion County Public Library System.)

ENTERING OCALA NATIONAL GAME REFUGE. Explorer William Bartram of Philadelphia wrote, "We traveled westward over a perfectly level plain, which appeared before and on each side of us, as a charming green meadow, thinly planted with low spreading pine trees. The upper stratum of the earth is a fine white crystalline sand, the very upper surface of which, being mixed or incorporated with the ashes of burnt vegetables, renders it of sufficient strength or fertility to clothe itself perfectly, with a very great variety of grasses, herbage and remarkably low shrubs, together with a very dwarf species of Palmetto." (Courtesy of State Library and Archives of Florida.)

AERIAL PHOTOGRAPHS OF THE FOREST. Remains of historic transportation routes (Volusia Trail, Churchill Road, and the Fort King Road) traverse the scrub regions; however, no associated historic sites have been recorded in the area. Any cultural expressions situated in the scrub are most likely of a brief, sporadic nature. (Both courtesy of Richard Mills.)

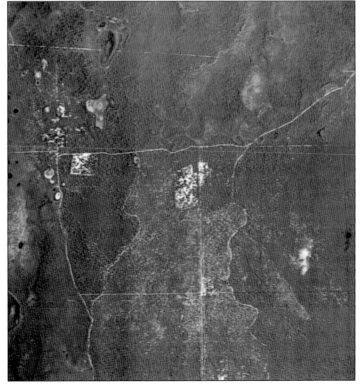

AERIAL PHOTOGRAPH. The Ocala National Forest, centrally located in peninsular Florida, is the southernmost of all forests in the National Forest System in the continental United States. Its boundaries encompass one of the most ecologically unique areas in the Southeastern United States. This photograph was taken in the 1930s. (Courtesy of Richard Mills.)

Hyacinth at St. Francis, St. Johns River. The *Hyacinth* was a stern-wheeled paddle steamer, registered number 96516, and belonged to Captain Harris. It was built in Jacksonville in 1900. It had a gross tonnage of 14 and a net of 5. It was 45 feet long, 9 feet wide, with a depth of 2 feet. St. Francis is now part of the Ocala National Forest and is located north of Crow's Bluff. (Courtesy of State Library and Archives of Florida.)

Water Hyacinth. In 1884, Mrs. W. F. Fuller obtained samples of the South American plant, the water hyacinth, at the World's Industrial and Cotton Centennial Exposition in New Orleans and planted them along the shore of her home on the St. Johns River. Within a decade, the water hyacinths covered an estimated 50 million acres of the river and its tributaries. Left uncontrolled in North American waters, water hyacinths can cover lakes and ponds, starving them of oxygen and thus killing fish and other organisms. (Courtesy of State Library and Archives of Florida.)

LIGHTFOOT PAVILION, ALEXANDER SPRINGS. Alexander Springs is located in a subtropical forest dominated by pine, oak, and Sabal palms. The large spring flows at 80 million gallons of crystal-clear water a day. (Courtesy of State Library and Archives of Florida.)

WALK TO THE BOIL, ALEXANDER SPRINGS, 1953. Discharging cool, clear freshwater at a rate of 107 cubic feet per second, Alexander Springs is one of the favorite destinations on the Florida Black Bear Scenic Byway, particularly during the warmer months when the springs become one of the region's favorite swimming holes. (Courtesy of State Library and Archives of Florida.)

TREADWAY ADMINISTRATION BUILDING, ALEXANDER SPRINGS. The springs are a major scuba site, as well as a stop on the Great Florida Birding Trail. Camping, snorkeling, and canoeing on the 7-mile spring run are available. A spur connects to the Florida National Scenic Trail. (Courtesy of State Library and Archives of Florida.)

THE MILL, JUNIPER SPRINGS, 1940. While never a mill to grind grain, the structure was built in the 1930s to provide electrical power for the Juniper Springs Campground. The building was constructed by the Civilian Conservation Corps (CCC) in 1935, as was the campground in an area of a sand-choked spring visited only by wildlife and an occasional hunter. (Courtesy of State Library and Archives of Florida.)

WATER WHEEL, JUNIPER SPRINGS, 1961.
Juniper Springs may be one of the clearest
streams in Florida. The springhead is
enclosed in a rock-and-concrete wall that
provides a large swimming pool. The water
flows out of the pool through a flume that
powers a waterwheel, which was once
used for generating electricity. The put-in
is a short distance below the waterwheel.
(Photograph by Stokes; courtesy of State
Library and Archives of Florida.)

THE MILL ACROSS THE SPRING, JUNIPER SPRINGS. The canoe trip from Juniper Springs Recreation
Area to Juniper Wayside flows about 7 miles through the heart of the Juniper Prairie Wilderness. On
the trip, a lush, tropical forest comprised of palms, cypress, and many kinds of southern hardwoods
surrounds visitors. The first 2.5 miles of this creek are narrow and winding, with a channel scarcely
wider than 6 feet. Past Half-Way Landing, the stream broadens out and becomes shallow and slow
moving. There are no intermediate access points, and the average family takes about four to five
hours to complete the trip. (Courtesy of State Library and Archives of Florida.)

BOY WITH DOG AND DEER, 1948.
As the most sought-after game
animal in North America, the
whitetail deer has always intrigued
both hunters and nonhunters
alike. Today the whitetail is the
most widespread deer in the
world. North America's whitetail
population is estimated at 20 to
25 million. (Courtesy of State
Library and Archives of Florida.)

MEN AND WOMEN ON FLOATS. Over
200 spring-fed lakes and rivers are
in the Ocala National Forest. Four
major springs are located within
the forest. Alexander, Salt, Juniper,
and Silver Glen Springs are all great
areas for swimming, snorkeling,
and spring diving. All the springs
have streams, which are ideal
for canoeing. (Courtesy of State
Library and Archives of Florida.)

SALT SPRINGS. Here visitors enjoy the Salt Springs. The park and areas adjacent to the springs were recently renovated, and the spring area is now bordered on three sides by a concrete wall and observation walkway that frames the pool in an open-ended rectangle, roughly 90 by 120 feet. The pool contains clear-blue water that, as a result of water rising to the surface through ancient salt deposits, contains a variety of minerals and rare trace elements, which gives it a mildly salty taste. The depth of the pool ranges from 2 to 5 feet in general, but is up to 20 feet deep at the spring vents/pits that are scattered in the enclosed end of the pool area. (Courtesy of State Library and Archives of Florida.)

OSPREY NEST IN THE SUNRISE. The osprey, or sea eagle, is a large bird of prey that is commonly seen circling above lakes, rivers, streams, and ponds or perched on dead trees (also known as "snags") or telephone poles. It is almost the size of an eagle and is dark brown with a white head and a brown mask from the eyes down to the cheeks. It also has a white and brown breast and underside. The osprey has large talons that allow it to fish by diving down and gripping onto fish. It is one of the most widespread birds in the world and is found on all continents except Antarctica. (Courtesy of State Library and Archives of Florida.)

RODMAN RESERVOIR.
Here is a boat ramp at Rodman Recreation Area in Ocala National Forest. The Rodman Reservoir, a 9,500-acre, 15-mile-long ecosystem, was created in 1968 when an earthen dam was built on the Ocklawaha River. It is located in Putnam County, just south of Palatka on Highway 19. (Courtesy of State Library and Archives of Florida.)

PADDLING AND FISHING, JUNIPER SPRINGS. Starting at the canoe ramp, the upper spring run is crystal clear and less than 1 foot deep. A white-sand bottom gives the appearance of paddling down a sandy, twisty, narrow roadway. Palmetto palms, oaks, and cypresses form almost a complete canopy over the small creek, which is much appreciated on hot summer days. About 2 miles downstream, the run enters Juniper Prairie Wilderness, a sanctuary for wildlife and those seeking to get far away from the urban world. The Florida Trail passes through here, offering a great place to hike as well as paddle. (Courtesy of State Library and Archives of Florida.)

GREEN TREE FROG "CALLING." Green tree frogs are drawn to open, damp areas like cattle tanks, pasture ponds, slowly-flowing canals, lakes, and streams, especially among emergent and floating vegetation. During the day, green tree frogs may be found resting on pond-side, emergent vegetation. The green tree frog call has been described as a series of "quonks" or as a "queenk-queenk-queenk" with a nasal inflection. Green tree frogs can be heard chorusing from early February to late summer in Florida, although in the more northerly parts of their range reproduction begins later in the spring. They call most frequently on warm, humid, overcast nights. Green tree frogs are one of the most common and abundant tree frogs in the Southeast. (Courtesy of State Library and Archives of Florida.)

VISITORS ENJOYING SALT SPRINGS. Open year-round, Salt Springs Recreational Area is at the heart of Salt Springs and is a major attraction for locals and visitors alike. In addition to camping, hiking, swimming, and various water recreational activities, the main attraction is the ancient subterranean springs that flow year-round at a constant temperature of 72 degrees and pump approximately 53 million gallons of crystal-clear water per day. (Courtesy of State Library and Archives of Florida.)

WOMEN SITTING ABOVE THE CRAB, SALT SPRINGS. The springs are home to an abundance of fish and marine life, which includes striped bass, mullet, and small fry. In addition, needlefish and blue crab may be seen, with crabs most commonly observed in the deeper portions of the spring openings. (Courtesy of State Library and Archives of Florida.)

SHOWING THEIR CRAB CATCH, SALT SPRINGS. Florida marine life was established at the site millennia ago when this portion of Florida was part of a shallow sea. When the land rose upward, the marine creatures remained at the site because of the salty flow from the spring. The bottom of the spring has exposed limestone, small rocks, and sand, as well as aquatic vegetation. (Courtesy of State Library and Archives of Florida.)

VIEW OF SWEETWATER SPRINGS, 1961. Sweetwater Springs is a second magnitude spring with a picturesque spring pool about 70 feet long by 60 feet wide. Clear, light-blue water flows from two oval-shaped vents about 4 to 5 feet long, with exposed limestone around the vents. Boils are visible over the vents. The discharge flows southward about 80 feet to Juniper Creek. (Photograph by Stokes; courtesy of State Library and Archives of Florida.)

VIEW OF JUNIPER SPRINGS, 1961. The 7-mile canoe run from Juniper Springs is one of the best canoeing opportunities in central Florida. The canopied creek winds through dense, primeval forests that seem untouched by man. A person can paddle through dappled light that filters through the trees down into crystalline water. At first glance, the run looks too narrow to navigate, but it grows in size steadily as it meanders past ancient cypress trees and lush semitropical forests. The narrow creek is filled with obstacles, and it takes some effort to avoid submerged snags and squeeze under overhanging branching. Whether one finds it fun or frustrating may depend on the canoeing skills. (Courtesy of State Library and Archives of Florida.)

PHEASANTS IN THE FOREST RESERVES, 1962. The pheasant is a large-sized bird that is found in fields and on the edge of woodlands, particularly in the Northern Hemisphere. Pheasants are best known for the brightly colored feathers (in a range of colors) and the long tail feathers of the male. The pheasant is thought to be native to Asia, with some relation to the wild chickens that are found in the jungles, particularly in India. Today the pheasant can be found all over the world, and there are more than 35 different species of pheasant today. Although the pheasant is not at immediate risk from extinction, pheasant populations are declining mainly due to loss of habitat and over-hunting. It is thought that around 80 percent of the pheasants hunted every year are only a few months old and are, therefore, unlikely to have mated with another pheasant. (Courtesy of State Library and Archives of Florida.)

CANOEING AT JUNIPER SPRINGS, 1966. Surrounded by the dryness of the Big Scrub, the world's largest scrub forest, Juniper Springs is a playground of hydrological wonders, with the center a jungle-like oasis of riotous growth. (Photograph by Johnson; courtesy of State Library and Archives of Florida and the U.S. Forest Service.)

WOMAN FEEDING A SQUIRREL. Squirrels are everywhere in Florida, from the coastal areas to inland lands. These incredibly agile, cute, and wacky characters are endearing to most, with the exception of only bird lovers, as sometimes squirrels will eat the seed they put out. Incredible climbers and jumpers, squirrels can hang from any angle it seems. (Courtesy of State Library and Archives of Florida.)

CAMPERS, 1961. The Ocala National Forest is a playground for naturalists, campers, fishermen, hikers, and off-road enthusiasts, covering 383,000-square acres, 67 miles of scenic hiking trails, and dozens of crystal-clear, spring-fed lakes and ponds. (Photograph by Stokes; courtesy of State Library and Archives of Florida.)

HUNTER RETURNING WITH A DEER, UMATILLA, 1957. Hunters gather around after successfully shooting a whitetail deer in Ocala National Forest near Umatilla. (Photograph by Charles Barron; courtesy of State Library and Archives of Florida.)

VIEW OF SILVER GLENN SPRINGS, 1958. Silver Glenn Springs's recreation area on State Road 19 was the site of the film *The Yearling.* Boating, swimming, fishing, or just plain relaxing are popular activities at the springs. (Photograph by Charles Barron; courtesy of State Library and Archives of Florida.)

ANOTHER VIEW OF SILVER GLENN SPRINGS, 1958. Silver Glen Springs is a first magnitude spring with a large, semicircular pool that measures 200 feet north to south and 175 feet east to west. Most of the strong flow emerges from two cavern openings in the rock at the bottom of the pool, with large boils at the water's surface over the vents. The vertical cave opening, called the Natural Well in the southwestern edge of the pool, is about 12 to 15 feet in diameter and 40 feet deep. The vent in the eastern part of the pool is a conical depression about 18 feet deep. Most of the spring pool has sand and limestone on the pool bottom, with areas of aquatic grasses. Large fresh and saltwater fish are common in the pool and around the vents. Additional flow is from sand boils in the bottom of the spring, which runs downstream from the head of the springs. (Photograph by Charles Barron; courtesy of State Library and Archives of Florida.)

VIEW OF WOODEN FOOTBRIDGE AT JUNIPER SPRINGS. Juniper Springs is surrounded by hardwood and saw palmetto forests, with ancient cypress trees along the spring run. In addition to the outflow of Juniper Springs, water is added to the run by adjacent Fern Hammock Springs and numerous small sand boils. (Courtesy of State Library and Archives of Florida.)

Silver Springs, hotel, and early glass bottom boat. Late 1880's

HOTEL AND EARLY GLASS-BOTTOM BOATS. This picture is from Silver Springs in the late 1880s. The glass-bottom boat was invented by a local youth, Philip Morrell, in a crude rowboat. In 1878, Hullam Jones built an advanced version and began rowing visitors around springs for a fee. In 1881, T. Brigham Bishop of New York City built a 200-room hotel near the main spring. In 1894 and 1895, a fire destroyed Bishop's hotel and he replaced it with a new inn called the Brown House. In the 1890s, commercial glass-bottom boats were developed. In 1898, H. L. Anderson purchased Silver Springs and the surrounding property. In 1909, C. (Ed) Carmichael bought 80 acres around the springs from Anderson for less than $3,000. He improved the comfort of the glass-bottom boats by installing cushioned seats and canopies. In 1924, Carl Ray and W. M. Davidson formed a partnership and bought the property surrounding the headwaters of the Silver River. In 1925, glass-bottom boats improved with the installation of gasoline engines; in 1932, they were converted to electric motors. By 1950, the number of guests at Silver Springs jumped to more than 800,000 a year. (Courtesy of Marion County Public Library System.)

JUNIPER SPRINGS, 1936. The Juniper Springs Recreation Area, the crown jewel of National Forest in Florida CCC recreation construction, has drawn the public since it was built in 1935. A limestone and wood mill house forms a picturesque backdrop for swimming, canoeing, and other fun. Restoration work sensitive to historical and rustic construction methods were planned for 2008. It is centrally located within the Ocala National Forest with an entrance on the north side of Highway 40. (Courtesy of Marion County Public Library System.)

DIVING INTO A SPRING, 1946. Surging from the Florida aquifer, clear, cold water literally "boils" up through the white sand. These waters fill the Juniper and Fern Hammock Springs at an amazing rate of 15 million gallons per day. This photograph shows numerous boils in the Fern Hammock Spring, which is at the end of the Juniper Nature Trail. Today no swimming or wading is allowed in this area to protect the fragile ecosystem. (Courtesy of State Library and Archives of Florida.)

JUNIPER SPRINGS, FERN HAMMOCK. Longleaf pines and Sabal palms provide a thick canopy over much of the campground. The subtropical scenery found at Juniper Springs is not found in any other National Forest in the United States. The combined daily water flow from the Juniper and Fern Hammock Springs is about 15 million gallons. The water temperature is a constant 72 degrees. (Courtesy of Marion County Public Library System.)

JUNIPER SPRINGS, 1928. From a January 10, 1937, *New York Times* article, "In the Ocala National Forest of spring and lake sprinkled Central Florida the United States Forest Service lately completed and opened as recreational areas Fern Hammock Springs and Juniper Springs. Juniper Springs, the newest development, is called a swimmer's paradise." (Courtesy of Marion County Public Library System.)

NEAR END OF NATURE TRAIL, FERN HAMMOCK. Given the diverse and numerous water sources present and an average rainfall of over 50 inches per year, the dry appearance of much of the forest may be surprising to the casual observer. This is due, however, to the high permeability and excessive drainage of the Astatula sands of the sand pine scrub and longleaf pine sandhills. (Courtesy of Marion County Public Library System.)

GRAHAMVILLE FERRY. The old road that runs through Hughes Islands to the Oklawaha River is known as the old Grahamville Road. Grahamville had the most-noted general store in Central Florida at the turn of the century in the days of the steamboat era when they were operating on the Oklawaha River. Grahamville doesn't exist anymore, but it was just a little bit southwest of the little settlement of Connor. Some of the old pilings where the old store stood are visible on the riverbanks. Some of the divers who were working this area said they made some fabulous finds there consisting of bottles of medicine, which had never been uncorked, and many other valuable artifacts. (Courtesy of Marion County Public Library System.)

Four

STEAMBOATS ON THE "SWEETEST WATER-LANE IN THE WORLD"

FROM THE 1830s TO THE 1890s. The forest was filled with passengers seeking the incredible views of primitive Florida. The boats moved along from the headwaters of the Silver River to the Ocklawaha and up to the St. Johns, where many of the passengers changed to open-water boats up to Jacksonville. The return trip was filled with more sojourners through the forest. Many people cleared the river of fallen trees and other obstructions and began to make the Ocklawaha trip with passenger steamboats at the close of the Civil War. Prior to this venture, nothing larger than barges propelled by poles navigated the waters. One time a ship took the bend too sharply at night and sunk. The high drama of the rivers provided many stories. (Courtesy of Gene Gallant.)

STEAMBOAT LANDING AND RAILWAY STATION. Who were the most well-known captains? How long were the trips? What were the accommodations like? How did the ships get built and put onto the river? What was it like on the river? How much did it change when railroads came? What was the demand for egret flumes and alligators? How much was the ticket? How was the trip at night? (Courtesy of Gene Gallant.)

Travel. Six decades of steam-propelled travel took place in the Ocala National Forest. Some of the most unusual vessels ever to traverse any waters were used on the river, known to many as a major destination in Florida. The river provided a twisting journey that slowed a vessel to a crawl, but it was worth the scenery viewed and the incredible reward at its end—Silver Springs. The channel width varied from 22 to 175 feet. In addition, logs, snags, overhanging trees, and accumulations of drift and aquatic vegetation often obstructed the Ocklawaha River. (Courtesy of Marion County Public Library System.)

On the Ocklawaha River, Fla.

TOP OF THE WATERWAYS. Leesburg, at the head of Lake Griffin 94 miles above the mouth, was generally regarded as the head of navigation, but light-draft steamboats and launches could pass through the lakes and connecting creeks and canals as far as Lake Apopka. Palatka was the normal head of navigation for steamboats using the St. Johns River, and service from Savannah was offered in the mid-1830s on a more or less regular basis, although it was often interrupted by wartime operations. In the early 1850s, service was offered from Charleston, and several crafts were running on the St. Johns River from Jacksonville to Enterprise and Mellonville, both on Lake Monroe. Of course, the advent of the Civil War and the Union invasions of the St. Johns area brought most of this steamboat traffic to a close. (Courtesy of Gene Gallant.)

Klawaha River Fla

RIVER IMPROVEMENTS. In 1830, Florida's population was noted to be 34,730. Largely, unknown, and somewhat unexplored below the area of present-day Orlando, the rivers, coastal waterways, and areas near the ocean were the centers of population. Northern Florida had an agricultural economy and comprised most of the Florida peninsula that was settled. (Courtesy of Gene Gallant.)

THE FIRST STEAMBOATS. In 1829, the first steamboats began service on the St. Johns and Apalachicola Rivers. Regular service was established on the St. Johns in the early 1830s, and the outbreak of the Second Seminole Indian War in December 1835 stimulated much activity as steamboats were employed to fulfill the logistical supply needs of the troops battling the elusive Seminoles. During the 1835–1842 war period, thousands of passages were made to and from Florida by steam-propelled vessels. Very few of these ever penetrated the Ocklawaha River, although Fort Brooke, some 32 river miles from the mouth, was established and undoubtedly supplied by water. After the war, efforts were increased to attract more settlers (including using land grants as bounties for war veterans). Travel to and within the state was largely by water, and steamships and steamboats provided much of the service. (Courtesy of Gene Gallant.)

LAND GRANTS. One of the after-effects of the Seminole War was the provision of land grants that were given as bonuses or bounties to participants in the conflict. This stimulated immigration, and greater reliance was placed on the steamboat, which became an aid to the development of Florida. By the 1850s, settlements were increasing on both coasts and along the St. Johns River. Pre-steamboat waterborne activities on the Ocklawaha were largely related to logging and the timber industry. Trees were cut along the river into logs that were placed together and then floated down to the St. Johns. They were transported to Jacksonville and were processed into lumber at the many sawmills and then put aboard sailing vessels for destinations along the Eastern Seaboard and abroad. Cedar was an especially valued lumber, and cypress was plentiful—both of which are scarce today. In time, southern pine would be a huge export. (Courtesy of Gene Gallant.)

FIRST COMMERCIAL VESSELS ON THE RIVER. Barges powered by poling were the first commercial vessels on the river. The barges would carry merchandise upstream to the region and downstream to market. The barge operations usually originated at Palatka and ended at a point on the Ocklawaha determined by water depth and demand. A gang of men, often slaves, propelled the barges, each equipped with a pole. This would be placed in the water at the bow, and the crew member would walk to the stern, pushing on the pole as he went. Arriving at the stern, the next man picked up the pole, walked to the bow, and planted the pole in the water again, repeating the process endlessly. The poles were also used to push the barge away from the riverbanks. About three weeks was required for the trip between Palatka and Silver Springs. Although the work was laborious and time-consuming, the small settlements near the river provided a source of trade for the barges that continued several years. (Courtesy of Gene Gallant.)

TWO PRINCIPAL PARTS. The river is divided into two parts. The first, and the most significant from a steamboat viewpoint, is from Silver Springs Run (also known as the Silver River) to the mouth of the Ocklawaha at the St. Johns River, slightly south of Welaka. The other part is from Silver Springs Run to Lake Griffin. A shallower part of the river, it was less and less frequented by steamboats as time went on. A common feature of both sections was the tortuous, always twisting path of the river. (Courtesy of Gene Gallant.)

RIVERBOATS. The initial direct references to boats on the river occur in the mid-1850s. In August of 1854, the barge *Ocklawaha* was launched at the Jacksonville shipyard of J. C. Butler. It was designated to ply on the river of its name from Welaka to Silver Springs. Another vessel, the *Fawn*, was launched in February 1855. (Courtesy of Silver River Museum.)

Captain Howard, "The Hart Line." Hubbard L. Hart was the developer and proprietor of the Hart Line of Ocklawaha River vessels. He was born in Guildford, Windham County, Vermont, on May 4, 1827, and his early life was spent on a farm there. Hart attended area grammar and high schools. When he was 21 years old, he came south in search of a business opportunity and spent three winters visiting various places along the Atlantic coast, even venturing to Cuba. (Courtesy of Silver River Museum.)

Harper's Magazine Story. Travel literature of the time was rife with accounts of journeys on the Ocklawaha vessels. *Harper's Magazine* described such a trip in its January 1876 issue, "Our comical little steamer, not unlike a dwarfed, two-storied canal-boat, had started out boldly from the Pilatka dock that morning with its full quota of twenty passengers on board, six feet of shelf having been carefully engaged in advance by letter or telegram for each person." (Courtesy of Gene Gallant.)

JAMES BURT. In 1860, Hart bought the *James Burt*. Little is known of it, but it was probably smaller than the Palatka-built *General Sumter*. It served an unknown length of time on the Ocklawaha River and inaugurated Hart's service. Hart's next vessel was the *Silver Spring* (73.91 tons, official Number 23066). During the war, Hart's vessels rendezvoused with the Confederate blockade runners and carried men and supplies up and down the Ocklawaha and St. Johns Rivers. (Courtesy of Marion County Public Library System.)

OKEEHUMKEE AT SILVER SPRINGS. In 1873, Colonel Hart constructed his *Okeehumkee* at his East Palatka (Hart's Point) shipyard. Destined to be an extremely long-lived vessel, it underwent considerable changes during its long tenure, all of which served to make it an improved, more useful vessel. Its name was also listed as *Okeehumkee II*, *Okahumpka*, *Okahumka*, and *Okeehumpkee*. It was reportedly named after a legendary Native American chief who lived around the area of the headwaters of the Ocklawaha lakes. A town in that area is also named Okahumpka. (Courtesy of Marion County.)

STEAMBOAT AND TRAIN. Over time, the emergence of the railroad and then the gasoline-powered craft in the 1910s and the 1920s signaled the end of steamboat activity. As Gene Gallant wrote, "The riverboats are long since gone: their paddle wheels stilled forever, their whistle blasts no longer heard reverberating through the wild swamp country of the Ocklawaha." (Courtesy of Marion County Public Library System.)

HAULING FUEL FOR THE STEAMBOAT. As early as 1835, Congress saw the need for improving the river and made its first provision to this end on February 24 of that year. Most of the improvements for steamboat purposes were made by the State of Florida because of the reluctance of the federal government to furnish the funds during the time needed. Long after the cessation of any steamboat travel, the federal government attempted to revive navigation by the proposed, then started, but not-to-be-completed Florida Cross State Barge Canal. This canal used the Ocklawaha for a considerable distance, and before the project was stopped, a considerable length of the lower river was dammed up. A new junction with the St. Johns River was created to the north of the natural junction. (Courtesy of Marion County.)

Five

TOWNS, FORTS, TRAILS, SINKHOLES, ISLANDS, AND BEAR HOLES

PAT'S ISLAND CEMETERY. Pat's Island, located in Juniper Prairie Wilderness, is one of the most popular historic attractions in the Ocala National Forest. The area was named after its first postmaster, Patrick Smith, who settled there in the 1840s, and it is known for its unique blend of two ecosystems, the longleaf pine and the sand pine scrub. Much of the land, bounded by the St. Johns and Ocklawaha Rivers, consists of the largest concentration of sand pine scrub in the world. Within this vast area, there are oases of fertile soils and moisture that support growth of longleaf pine, wiregrass, turkey oak, and other trees and plants not found in the surrounding arid scrub. Pioneers who settled in these areas called them islands, because a sea of scrub surrounded them. Smith ran his little post office in the front room of his home, which was just north of the large sinkhole. A sinkhole is caused by a collapse of the upper strata of limestone rock into either an underground channel of water or into an empty underground cavern that has been vacated by water. These sinkholes are found all over the forest and form the basis of many of the lakes. The springs are formed where an underground flow of water has enough pressure to bring it to the surface, forming a stream. Pictured is Nancy Brower (with the notepad) talking to Richard Mills. (Courtesy of Richard Mills.)

MARION COUNTY ROAD. The Ocala National Forest receives more visitors than any other national forest in the Sunshine State. Millions annually visit the forest, which is one of Central Florida's last remaining traces of forested land. The Ocala National Forest contains a high proportion of remaining Florida scrub habitat and is noted for its sand pine scrub ecosystem. (Courtesy of Marion County.)

ABUNDANT PINES. The forest contains the largest concentration of sand pine in the world as well as some of the best remaining stands of longleaf pine in Central Florida. (Courtesy of Richard Mills)

TRAIL/ROAD. In the 1920s, what is now State Road 19 through the Ocala National Forest on the west side of St. Johns River was little more than a rutted trail, much like many roads throughout the county before an extensive road-building program began. (Courtesy of Richard Mills.)

HORSEBACK RIDING TRAILS IN THE FOREST. Forest riding trails are actually old roads 6 to 8 feet wide, marked at intervals with painted spots—called blaze—on the trees. Some of the best trails include the One Hundred Mile Trail and the LAM Trail. (Courtesy of Richard Mills.)

TRAIL/ROAD. The Florida Trail in the Ocala National Forest is certified as a Florida National Scenic Trail (FNST) and has been called the "crown jewel" of the Florida trail system. The entire length of the trail in the national forest is also designated as part of the Florida Statewide Greenways and Trails System. (Courtesy of Richard Mills.)

FLORIDA TRAIL. The trail traverses a range of natural communities, including extensive stands of longleaf pines and scattered communities of sand pines, other short leaf pines, and hardwoods. The trail also skirts open prairies and ponds that are excellent for viewing wildlife. (Courtesy of U.S. Forest Service.)

DAYTONIA HIGHWAY NEAR THE LAKE BRYANT RAILROAD STATION. The forest's porous roads and largely underdeveloped character provide an important recharge for the Floridan Aquifer. (Courtesy of Marion County Public Library System.)

FROM HALF-MOON TOWER LOOKING NORTHEAST, 1928. The Big Scrub, as it is affectionately known, is the world's largest stand of sand pine scrub forest. It also contains one of the most scenic extensions of the FNST. (Both courtesy of Marion County Public Library System.)

ROAD IN A WOODED AREA. Big, unbroken acreages of sand pine are a great habitat for whitetail deer. Although coniferous trees never lose their leaves, they do shed them. This blankets the forest floor with a thick bed of pine needles. Deer use this blanket to their advantage. (Photograph by Wallace Hughes; courtesy of State Library and Archive of Florida.)

FIRE LINE, 1929. Created by road graders, fire lines are critical in wildland firefighting, because without them a fire could quickly get out of control. By depriving the fire of fuel, a fire line slows the advance of a blaze and confines it to a specific area, which can make it much easier to control. Typically fire lines are made by churning up the earth with shovels or bulldozers. Sometimes firefighters take advantage of roads and paths in the way of a fire, using them as firebreaks rather than trying to cut fresh fire lines. A fire line can also be made with the use of a controlled burn, which consumes the fuel in an area before the fire has a chance to reach it. (Photograph by C. H. Coulter; courtesy of State Library and Archive of Florida.)

A Road in Ocala National Park. The 360,000-acre Ocala National Forest was the first designated national forest east of the Mississippi River. (Courtesy of State Library and Archive of Florida.)

Dirt Road, 1967. The Florida Trail in the Ocala National Forest offers mostly level, dry hiking through pine islands and hardwood forests along the edges of prairies and ponds. In the southern portion of the forest, the trail crosses some narrow sections of hardwood swamp. (Courtesy of State Library and Archive of Florida.)

EXPLORING THE FOREST. Experience crystalline waters emerging from the midst of the world's largest scrub forest, or hike an easy nature trail and boardwalk in the Ocala National Forest. (Courtesy of State Library and Archive of Florida.)

NATURE'S AQUARIUM. The CCC constructed Juniper Springs in the mid-1930s, boasting semitropical scenery not found in any other national forest in the continental United States. The combined daily water flow from Juniper and Fern Hammock Springs is about 13 million gallons. The water temperature is a constant 72 degrees. (Courtesy of State Library and Archive of Florida.)

VIEW OF THE LODGE ACROSS THE SPRING. At Juniper Springs, there are several types of Florida springs, which include the following: massive outpourings from a cavern at the headspring, tiny bubblers along the bottom of the run, constant seeps along the loamy slopes, eerie flat boils, and giant boils thrusting perpetual clouds of sand skyward. (Courtesy of State Library and Archive of Florida.)

V. J. ALLEN JR.'S HOME, RAINBOW SPRINGS. V. J. Allen Jr. was the former operations manager of Rainbow Springs. He purchased a lease on The Motor Lodge from Thomas L. Barrett of St. Petersburg. Rock City and Ruby Falls leased the sightseeing boats and operations with interests from Kenneth S. Keyes of Miami. Allen's lease was to run for 7.5 years and consisted of the main lodge and 29 rental units. Earlier, Allen managed Silver Glen Springs in the Ocala National Forest and had been waterfront manager of Wakulla Springs, Florida. (Courtesy of State Library and Archive of Florida.)

KERR HOUSE HOTEL, KERR CITY. Lake Kerr, which is in the heart of what is now Ocala National Forest, and Kerr City were named after Robert B. Kerr. They are located off County Route 316, approximately 3 miles west of Salt Springs. Kerr City is a wonderfully preserved ghost town, which is listed on the National Register of Historic Places. Covering 205 acres, Kerr City was the second town platted in Marion County in 1884 and grew to 100 residents in its day. Originally a cotton plantation during the Civil War, Kerr City flourished as an orange-growing community for a number of years and served as a stagecoach stop for travelers commuting from the St. Johns River to Ocala. Original structures included a hotel, sawmill, general store, pharmacy, post office, school and church, and numerous Victorian-style homes. The 1925 gas station in town is the oldest Texaco station in the state of Florida still in operation. (Courtesy of State Library and Archive of Florida.)

SILVER SPRINGS HOTEL. The natural beauty of the area and the colorful lifestyle of these rugged people fascinated writer Marjorie Kinnan Rawlings. The Pulitzer Prize–winning author of *Cross Creek* lived much of her life in Micanopy. Her stories and descriptions captured the primitive, sublime beauty of the forest. She stayed with the last two inhabitants of the island, Calvin and Mary Long, in October 1933. During this stay and other visits, she recorded many stories told by the Longs. Calvin's childhood story of nursing a deer from a fawn gave her the idea for the Pulitzer Prize–winning novel *The Yearling*. The book was made into a movie that starred Gregory Peck, Jane Wyman, and Claude Jarman Jr. and was filmed on location in the early 1940s. (Courtesy of State Library and Archive of Florida.)

DIRECTOR CLARENCE BROWN AND *THE YEARLING* TECHNICAL EXPERTS ON LOCATION. The Pat's Island sinkhole was used as a water supply by the early settlers and was mentioned in the book *The Yearling*. In the book, one of Jody's (character) problems was the fact that the only water available at Pat's Island (it was called Baxter's Island in the book) was the water that was down in the bottom of the sinkhole. The Boils Trail at the glen is where Jody built a "flutter mill" with palmetto leaves and sticks. (Courtesy of Marion County Public Library System.)

JODY FEEDING THE FAWNS. Claude Jarman Jr., who starred as Jody in the movie version of *The Yearling*, is shown here on location near Silver Springs when the film was being made. (Courtesy of Mozert Studio.)

RICHARD MILLS, HISTORIAN.
David Cook, Richard Mills, Gene
Gallant, and others have provided
many articles and books on Marion
County and Ocala National Forest
history. (Photograph by author.)

RICHARD MILLS AND ROB NORMAN. This picture was taken at the home of local historian
Richard Mills (left) with the author of this book, Dr. Robert A. Norman (right). (Photograph
by Ibsen A. Morales.)

THE HOMESITE ON PAT'S ISLAND, SOUTH OF THE SINKHOLE. The trees around the house were used as landmarks in the book *The Yearling*, especially the old chinaberry that stood by one of the corners of the house. The road from Pat's Island ran east and south. The old road from the island ran east and a little bit to the south across Juniper Creek and between Sweetwater and the highway. The remains of the old bridge are still visible on the creek. Following the St. Johns River, the road continued to Volusia, near what is now Astor. In the book, characters made this trip by foot several times, because they had relatives and friends that lived in Volusia. The book opens with Jody making a flutter mill at the glen, which refers to Silver Glen Springs. The flutter mill was constructed on privately owned land at the end of State Route 19. The road through Pat's Island, running from east to west, used to be the main road from Lake George to Ocala. (Courtesy of Richard Mills.)

1890s Houses. The Reuben Long family came to the area around 1872, and individual family members applied for and were granted homestead acres that they worked and lived on for many years. Human habitation on the island peaked before the turn of the 20th century, which was when about a dozen families sought to eke out a living on the 1,400-acre island. A living was made from farming, running cattle and hogs, hunting, fishing, making moonshine whisky, and trading with boat travel on the St. Johns River. (Both courtesy of Marion County.)

SCHOOL PHOTOGRAPHS. There is an ecological uniqueness of this longleaf pine island that is surrounded by scrub pine, which creates a single community isolated from the mainstream of Central Florida life. The imposed remoteness contributed to an island untouched by outside forces. The community had its own church, school, post office, and self-appointed lay ministers. Life was hard on the island, and after the big back-to-back freezes of 1894 and 1895, the population began to decline. Most of the settlers had sold or leased their homesteads before the Ocala National Forest was formed in 1908. In 1935, the island was abandoned by man and surrendered back to the elements after less than 100 years of human occupation. (Both courtesy of Marion County.)

VISIT PAT'S ISLAND VIA THE YEARLING TRAIL. The trailhead is located on State Route 19 across from the Silver Glen Springs entrance. From there, visitors hike for 6 miles and are able to see various sites of historical significance while enjoying the natural beauty of the island. (Courtesy of Richard Mills.)

LAKE KERR. Lake Kerr area has a great deal of history. Robert B. Kerr was a surveyor back in 1835 who surveyed around this lake. He had been warned many times by the Native Americans to leave the surveying and get out. He refused; however, his decision to stay quickly changed when an arrow missed his head by inches. After this incident, he gave thanks for being alive, named the body of water Lake Kerr after himself, and then left until after the Seminole Indian War was over. (Courtesy of Marion County Public Library System.)

MILES TO OCALA. Salt Springs and Alexander Springs are part of the Great Florida Birding Trail. Included in the forest is more than a 50-mile section of the Florida National Scenic Trail. The Paisley Woods Bicycle Trail is a challenging 22-mile-long ride through live oak hammocks, grassy prairies, and pinelands. The Ocala One Hundred Mile Horse Trail consists of three sections through sand pine scrub, longleaf pinelands, and grassy prairies. (Courtesy of Marion County.)

Six

TURPENTINE CAMPS

TURPENTINE CAMPS. The Ocala Forest was home to numerous turpentine camps. The growth of the naval stores industry was rapid in Florida in the early 1900s, and the pine tree provided the raw material. The products of the naval stores industry were the oils, resins or gums, and tars of pine trees, particularly the longleaf and slash pine. The naval stores refers to products that were essential parts of a wooden ship's stores and included tar, pitch, spars, and masts. Crude gum, which was not soluble in water, sealed cracks between the wooden planks of a ship. When the gum was cooked to form pitch, a better means of caulking a vessel or waterproofing various objects was obtained. A good seal meant the difference between life and death for many sailors. (Courtesy of Marion County Public Library System.)

TURPENTINE WORKERS AND BUSINESS OWNER. By 1700, the long-bitted ax was used for cutting the box, or cavity, in the base of the tree to collect the gum. The major problem with the boxing method was the increased formation of scrape on the face of the tree, as the height of the face had to be increased during the weekly chipping process. The so-called virgin dip, or the finest gum, could only be produced in the first year the tree was worked. When the French system came along, which was adapted later in the United States, cups were used to collect the gum. The cups could be raised periodically, reducing the formation of scrape. This method was far less destructive for the timber. Some of the tools were the hack and puller, which were used for the weekly chipping process, and the long-handled, flat, oval-shaped dip iron, which was used to remove the gum from the cavity. The dippers carried wood-dip buckets to collect the gum. Early dip wagons were usually two-wheeled carts pulled by oxen with a dip crew dipping or extracting down from the box. (Courtesy of Marion County.)

TURPENTINE HANDS AT WORK. Often a common ax was initially used as a chipping tool in the gum or scrape extraction process. Whatever could be used to renew the flow of gum from the tree was utilized. Tool manufacturers eventually took over production, and standardized hacks and pullers were developed after 1850. Early attempts at timber conservation, including prohibiting boxing any trees that were too small, were defeated. The timber was abandoned after about five years, creating a 50 percent mortality rate. The remaining timber was chopped down for wood. The area became an almost-treeless monument to the destructive methods of turpentine harvest. (Courtesy of Marion County.)

TURPENTINE STILL. The site of the still was determined primarily by the location of the timber to be worked, the water supply, and the transportation. Access to the roads, rivers, or railroads was crucial to transport the distillation products to markets. Roads were quite limited and access was primitive. Great quantities of water were required to fill the large cypress wood tubs that were used to cool and condense the hot distillate vapors. Rivers and bays provided the most convenient and effective ways for direct transportation of turpentine and rosin to market. Eventually there were central stills developed as highly specialized plants. Each plant employed chemists and other highly trained engineers and technicians. The largest central stills processed as many as 30,000 units and had storage facilities for 40,000 to 50,000 barrels of gum. Eventually the small fire stills were unable to compete, and by 1960 the last commercially operated fire still closed. (Courtesy of Marion County.)

MAJOR USES OF TURPENTINE. A rapidly growing market arose in fragrance chemicals derived from turpentine, along with products for laundry cleaning, furniture polish and shoe polish, candles, liquid floor wax, and as a solvent for paint and varnish. A typical home at the time used turpentine to fight infections, relieve soreness, and aid in the healing of cuts and bruises. It was used for insect bites, athlete's foot, snakebites, croup and sore throats, and to keep nasty insects away. In the 1920s, rosin oils, greases, and printing ink accounted for up to 25 percent of the total consumption of rosin. Lampblack, used in India ink and lithography, was produced by the combustion of rosin in furnaces. The demand for rosin was initially minimal, but by the 1930s it was used extensively in paper, soap, and varnish products. The pharmaceutical and chemical industry in the 1940s began to use turpentine for disinfectants, medicated pine tar soap, and shampoos, salves, and therapeutic oils. (Courtesy of Marion County Public Library System.)

Seven

LOGGING AND TRAINS

CYPRESS LOGS, MARION COUNTY LUMBER INDUSTRY. There is still evidence of early logging with the large cypress stumps along the river. Williston Cypress Company owned the area south of Alco Dock, and operations ceased in the early 1930s. The resulting deforestation and other poor management practices, such as over-burning areas, deep-chipping for turpentine, tapping trees that were too small, and ranging stock in areas where seedlings were trying to grow, wiped out the very foundation of local economies. Market value of much of the property dropped so low that property taxes became higher than the actual monetary value of the land. Due to laxity of earlier tax laws, property taxes were not paid, and local economies suffered from the loss of revenue. These conditions stimulated the formation of national forests throughout the Southern United States, with the earliest in Florida proclaimed in 1908 and the latest in 1936. (Courtesy of Marion County.)

FLOATING TIMBER ON OCKLAWAHA RIVER. The cutting crews lived on a barge or "shantyhouse" as it was known. They arrived about two years in advance of the felling crews and would take axes and girdle the 4- and 5-foot-diameter cypress trees to the heart of the wood. They would then let the trees stand until they dried out, which was usually at least a year. Then the felling crews would come in then with crosscut saws and fell the trees. The dried trees would float like a cork. (Courtesy of Marion County.)

CYPRESS TREES MARKED FOR LOGGING. When the Civil War ended, Hubbard L. Hart immediately opened negotiations with the State of Florida and soon had a contract to clear the Ocklawaha River of all stumps, logs, snags, and surface obstructions. Soon Hart's steamboats were operating at full capacity on the river. (Courtesy of Marion County.)

TIMBERING. Prior to the formation of national forests in the Southern United States, many local communities were dependent upon the turpentine and timber industries. Although these industries started earlier in some places than others, the height of its importance was generally from about 1890 to 1920. (Courtesy of Marion County.)

MEN COLLECTING SALVAGE TIMBER. Sam Griffis (right), salvage timber operator since the 1930s, is removing lightning-struck or bug-infested trees. (Courtesy of State Library and Archives of Florida.)

LOGGING WITH OXEN. After 1915, part-time employment in these industries began to decline, and by the 1930s this type of occupation was scarce compared to what it once was. This continued until the end of World War II. Its decline was a direct effect of poor management of timber resources. (Courtesy of Marion County.)

TRANSPORTING LOGS BY MULE CARAVAN. Usually the pines were first tapped for turpentine products. When they were "worked out," meaning so much of the sap had been removed that tree breakage and disease began, the trees were cut for timber. These two operations were carried out by different companies, but sometimes the same operator did both. The forests were viewed as a resource to be used as hard and as quickly as possible according to the flux of the market. When timber prices went up, every tree with market value was cut. (Courtesy of Marion County.)

MILL. The logging parties came in by tugboat, with steam-driven winches that allowed the logs to be pulled to the river. The logs were then formed into large rafts, which were then towed by the tugboat or freely drifted downstream to the large mill at Palatka. (Courtesy of Marion County.)

SAWMILL. After all the timber was removed from the shores of the large rivers and tributary streams leading into the St. Johns River, the mill at Palatka went out of operation between 1935 and 1940. Since then, smaller mills cut the small patches that the large operations overlooked. The end result is that on the Ocala, along the St. Johns River Valley, no merchantable hardwood remains. It takes a very long period of time for hardwoods to make a comeback. (Courtesy of Marion County.)

LOGGING TRAIN. The Dow Jones Industrial Average is a well-known market indicator today, based on the stock prices of 30 large companies, which includes Wal-Mart and Walt Disney. The original Dow Index, published in 1884, had just 12 members, and 11 of them were railroad companies. (Courtesy of Marion County.)

GROWTH OF THE OCALA, SILVER SPRINGS REGION. An increase of railroad transportation to the area in the late 19th century spurred the region's growth. A new line, the Ocala Northern Railroad (ONRR), leased the 1.9-mile SAL spur to Silver Springs on December 14, 1909, and obtained trackage rights over 4 miles of the SAL to downtown Ocala. The ONRR was owned by E. P. Rentz, who owned a sawmill at Silver Springs. He soon built it north to Fort McCoy and constructed a logging railroad west into the forest. He continued to build the ONRR, and it reached Palatka by 1912, with 45.5 miles of track from Silver Springs to Palatka. Plans to extend the railroad across the St. Johns River to Hastings and then north on the east shore to Jacksonville fell through; the company went bankrupt in May 1913. The railroad was also involved with the Ocala Southwestern Railroad, which was planned to travel to Tampa; however, no part of that was ever constructed. (Courtesy of Silver River Museum.)

NO. 113. SILVER SPRING HOTEL FLA.

RAILROAD. The Ocklawaha Valley Railroad is one of the most interesting railroads in Florida's history and connected with the Seaboard, Southern, Atlantic Coast Line, and the Florida East Coast Railroads. Besides Jacksonville Terminal Company, no other railroad connected with all four of Florida's major rail lines. (Courtesy of Silver River Museum.)

TRANSPORTATION. Other forms of transportation beyond steamboats were helping to move goods and people. In the early 1900s, Silver Springs provided steamboat travel to Palatka, automobile travel to Ocala, and railroad travel to many Florida locations. (Courtesy of Silver River Museum.)

Eight

CRACKER COWBOYS

AN OXCART IN OCALA. Florida has a history of thriving businesses in horses and cattle. Spaniard explorer Ponce de León discovered Florida in 1513. When he returned in 1521, he brought horses and seven Andalusian cattle, the ancestors of the Texas Longhorns, which turned Florida into America's oldest cattle-raising state. The St. Augustine missionaries and Spanish settlers who raised beef had to also fight Native American raids, mosquitoes, cattle fever ticks, storms, swamps, and snakes. Despite the harsh conditions, there were already dozens of ranches along the Florida Panhandle and the St. Johns River before 1700. (Courtesy of Marion County.)

A "TYPICAL" OXCART. Florida's landscape was once a vast area for livestock pastures. Most Florida settlers raised beef for food and moved south with the cattle through Alachua County into the Kissimmee Valley and on to Lake Okeechobee to search for new pastures. The beef industry grew as railroads that could ship cattle spread into Florida. More people arrived from other states, and new towns sprang up around the ranches. Blacksmiths, shopkeepers, cowboys, and others lived in these settlements. (Courtesy of Marion County.)

Nine

SILVER SPRINGS

ACTIVITIES ON THE WATER. Silver Springs was the principal destination of the travelers who braved the Ocklawaha 150 years ago. Daniel Brinton was one of the first to bring the glories of Silver Springs to the attention of the world and recorded his observations in 1859. He asserted, "To be appreciated in its full beauty, it should be approached from the Ocklawaha." He had taken more than a week traversing the "dark and crooked river" in a pole barge "wearied with the monotony of the dark and gloomy forests that everywhere shade its inky stream. When one bright morning, a sharp turn [revealed] the pellucid waters of the Silver Springs Run." Silver Springs is the largest limestone artesian spring formation in the world. With an average output of 800 million gallons a day, the early Native Americans considered them sacred and paid homage to them with elaborate ceremonies. Scientists have discovered evidence of human activity dating back 100 centuries. Certainly this is one of Florida's oldest attractions. There are a host of activities to enjoy, such as the world-famous glass-bottom boat tours. (Courtesy of Marion County Public Library System.)

GARY COOPER IN *DISTANT DRUMS*. Silver Springs is one of Florida's oldest attractions. Numerous movies and television shows attracted by the extraordinary clarity have done underwater filming in this location. *Distant Drums* depicts the Second Seminole War (1835–1842) in Florida. The true star of the film is the scenery, which shows off the beautiful Ocala National Forest wilderness. (Courtesy of Warner Brothers Pictures Distributing Corporation.)

WATER SCENE IN *DISTANT DRUMS*. The film was made in 1951 and the cast included Gary Cooper as Capt. Quincy Wyatt, Mari Aldon as Judy Beckett, Richard Webb as Lt. Richard Tufts, Ray Teal as Private Mohair, Arthur Hunnicutt as a monk, and Robert Barrat as Gen. Zachary Taylor. (Courtesy of Warner Brothers Pictures Distributing Corporation.)

ROSS ALLEN MILKING A SNAKE. Ross Allen, a noted herpetologist, founded the Silver Springs Reptile Institute. Allen pioneered many forms of snake antivenom, including a dried variety. He also imported and supplied venoms for medical purposes and biochemical research. (Photograph by Ken Goodman; courtesy of Wild Animal Pictures, Inc.)

ROSS ALLEN LIFTING A TURTLE. Ross Allen Island features a collection of native snakes, turtles, arachnids, otters, and other animals found in Florida. The exhibit also showcases archival photographs and information on the world-famous naturalist Ross Allen. (Photograph by Ken Goodman; courtesy of Wild Animal Pictures, Inc.)

LADY HOLDING A SNAKE AND ROSS ALLEN WRESTLING A SNAKE UNDERWATER. Marjorie Kinnan Rawlings, author of *The Yearling* and *Cross Creek*, overcame her fear of snakes after Allen took her on a snake hunt in Florida's cattle country. In *Cross Creek*, she described the rattlesnake hunt as follows: "The hunting ground was Big Prairie, south of Arcadia and west of the northern tip of Lake Okeechobee. Big Prairie is a desolate cattle country, half marsh, and half pasture, with islands of palm trees, cypress, and oaks. At that time of year, the cattlemen and Native Americans were burning the country, on the theory that the young fresh wire grass that springs up from the roots after a fire is the best cattle forage. Ross planned to hunt his rattlers in the forefront of the fires. He said, 'they lived in the winter in gopher holes, coming out in the midday warmth to forage, and would move ahead of the flames and be easily taken.' " (Both courtesy of Silver River Museum.)

WRESTLING AN ALLIGATOR UNDERWATER. Ross Allen's Alligator Town was to be a tourist attraction and alligator farm in Lake City near the intersection of I-75 and U.S. 90. Rather than fight Disney, Ross hoped to siphon off some of its southbound traffic on the way. (Courtesy of Silver River Museum.)

KIDS ON AN ALLIGATOR. Waterslides, rides, and other theme-park trappings were to be added eventually to Alligator Town with an amphitheater for concerts and other shows. Allen and business partner Dennis Magee, a former president of the Florida Herpetological Society, planned a June 1981 opening. (Photograph by Ken Goodman; courtesy of Wild Animal Pictures, Inc.)

ROSS ALLEN, 1934. The 50-acre, $800,000 Alligator Town was to feature a reptile museum, an alligator farm with underwater alligator wrestling, a rattlesnake show, turtle garden, and a wild lizard jungle. (Courtesy of Silver River Museum.)

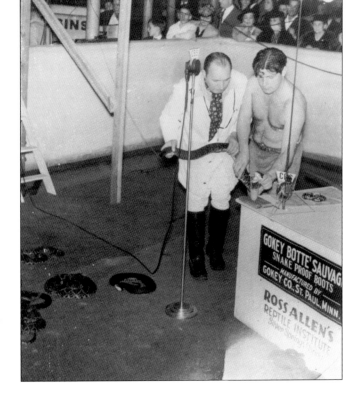

SHOW. Ross Allen demonstrates how venom is extracted from a rattlesnake. Venom was not the only product of the institute. Rattlesnake meat in supreme sauce was canned by Allen and sold in gourmet shops in many cities. (Courtesy of Silver River Museum.)

WRESTLING A SAWFISH. Born in Pennsylvania in 1908, Ross Allen appeared in several short films. He owned and operated the Ross Allen Reptile Institute in Silver Springs from 1929 until 1969. When he started this tourist attraction, Allen also asked local Seminole Indians to set up a village, demonstrate their traditional skills, and sell their crafts. His work gradually focused on scientific observation, research, and publications. (Courtesy of Silver River Museum.)

TANGLED SNAKE AND ROSS ALLEN. On the 1960s television show *What's My Line?*, Allen explained that one reason why he became an expert in milking rattlesnake venom was because the venom was needed to treat his son's illness and there was a shortage. (Courtesy of Silver River Museum.)

ROSS ALLEN IN HIS LATER YEARS.
In the 1970s, the success of Walt
Disney World in Orlando hurt
attendance at smaller tourist
destinations throughout Florida,
including Ross Allen's. He
planned to locate his last tourist
attraction, Alligator Town, close
to I-75 and Disney traffic, but he
died a month prior to the park's
opening in June 1981. In his
honor, the largest island in Silver
Springs was renamed Ross Allen
Island in January 2000. (Courtesy
of Silver River Museum.)

THE FLORIDA REPTILE INSTITUTE. For nearly
50 years, Ross Allen owned and operated the
Ross Allen Reptile Institute at Silver Springs,
which contained an extensive collection of
snakes, crocodilians, and animals from around
the world. (Courtesy of Silver River Museum.)

SNAKE GOING FOR THE BOOT. Internationally, Ross Allen was known for his wild animal business, the development of antivenom, and other research about reptiles. At one time, his wild animal business was located in downtown Ocala. He provided animals for a number of movies filmed in this area. (Courtesy of Silver River Museum.)

ALLIGATOR WRESTLING. Although not a trained herpetologist, Allen was one of the first to document the natural behavior of the American alligator. He capitalized on the public's fascination with not only alligators, but also snakes and the Florida critters at his popular reptile show. (Courtesy of Silver River Museum.)

TURTLES AND FISH. Since 1916, film crews have been attracted to "Florida's Original Tourist Attraction" when the silent movie *The Seven Swans*, starring Richard Barthelmess and Marguerite Clark, was shot at the park. Many more small films followed, but it wasn't until the 1930s and 1940s that the exotic surroundings of Ocala became a popular location for films. Between 1932 and 1942, Johnny Weissmuller starred in six *Tarzan* movies that were all shot at Silver Springs. (Courtesy of Silver River Museum.)

FILMING. Between 1958 and 1961, more than 100 episodes of *Sea Hunt*, starring Lloyd Bridges, were filmed at Silver Springs. That television series, the horror movie *Creature From The Black Lagoon*, National Geographic specials, and numerous television shows and commercials have been shot at Silver Springs over the years. When television became popular in the early 1950s, Silver Springs continued as a location for national television talk shows and adventure series. Some of the shows filmed there have been *The Jack Paar Show, You Asked For It, I Spy, Mutual of Omaha's Wild Kingdom, SeaQuest*, and the soap opera *One Life To Live*. (Courtesy of Silver River Museum.)

FILMING UNDERWATER. Since the 1940s, many movies have been shot in and around Silver Springs's main spring area. Some of them include *The Yearling*, starring Gregory Peck and Jane Wyman; *Distant Drums*, with Gary Cooper; *Underwater*, starring Jane Russell and Richard Egan; *Blindfold*, with Rock Hudson and Claudia Cardinale; *Never Say Never Again*, starring Sean Connery; and *Smokey and the Bandit Part 3*, with Jackie Gleason. Military training films on jungle warfare have also been shot at the park. (Courtesy of Silver River Museum.)

MOVIES AND TELEVISION SHOWS. Many people who filmed and produced movies and television shows have been attracted to the area because of its extraordinarily clear water in which underwater filming could be done. Countless television specials and commercials have also been shot at the park. The Discovery Channel, Mercury Motors, Johnson & Johnson, DuPont, and Dean Witter have all filmed shows or commercials at the springs. (Courtesy of Silver River Museum.)

The Ocala National Forest

The visitor's centers provide a wonderful overview and an excellent selection of nature and forest educational material, maps, and area brochures. The hours are 9:00 a.m. to 5:00 p.m. daily. The centers are located along State Route 19, seven miles south of Alexander Springs (Seminole District); along State Route 19 in Salt Springs (Lake George District); and along the western boundary at Highway 40 and County Route 315 (District boundary).

Lake George Ranger District
17147 East Highway 40
Silver Springs, Florida 34488
Phone: (352) 625-2520
http://www.southernregion.fs.fed.us/florida

For Maps of the Forest:
http://www.trails.com